An Imprint of Pop!
popbooksonline.com

Living through American History

Living through the REVOLUTIONARY WAR

by Grace Hansen

WELCOME TO DiscoverRoo!

This book is filled with videos, puzzles, games, and more! Scan the QR codes* while you read, or visit the website below to make this book pop.

popbooksonline.com/rev-war-life

abdobooks.com
Published by Pop!, a division of ABDO, PO Box 398166, Minneapolis, Minnesota 55439.

Printed in the United States of America, North Mankato, Minnesota.

052023
092023

Cover Photo: Library of Congress - *Evacuation Day and Washington's Triumphant Entry*
Interior Photos: Granger Image Collection; Library of Congress; Shutterstock Images; Alamy
Editor: Elizabeth Andrews
Series Designer: Laura Graphenteen; Neil Klinepier

Library of Congress Control Number: 2022950560

Publisher's Cataloging-in-Publication Data
Names: Hansen, Grace, author.
Title: Living through the Revolutionary War / by Grace Hansen
Description: Minneapolis, Minnesota : Pop!, 2024 | Series: Living through American history | Includes online resources and index
Identifiers: ISBN 9781098244330 (lib. bdg.) | ISBN 9781098245030 (ebook)
Subjects: LCSH: United States--History--Revolution, 1775-1783--Juvenile literature. | Political science--History--18th century--Juvenile literature. | Social history--Juvenile literature.
Classification: DDC 973.2--dc23

*Scanning QR codes requires a web-enabled smart device with a QR code reader app and a camera.

TABLE OF CONTENTS

CHAPTER 1

ROAD TO REVOLUTION

Great Britain ruled the 13 North American colonies from 1607 to 1775. Life in the colonies was hard. Colonists grew food, built homes, made clothing, and did many other jobs. But by the mid-1700s, colonial life was becoming easier.

WATCH A VIDEO HERE!

The 13 colonies were very different from one another. Each of the colonies had its own government. The colonies traded with one another but were not officially connected.

Colonists worked hard to settle Jamestown, the first permanent English colony in North America.

Colonists were angered by the taxes that came with the Stamp Act of 1765.

Around 1763, issues began to arise. King George III and the British Parliament had forced new **taxes** and trade restrictions on the colonies. Many colonists wanted more independence from Great Britain.

King George III ruled the United Kingdom of Great Britain and Ireland until his death in 1820.

7

The Declaration of Independence was signed in 1776 by 56 delegates who represented the colonies.

In 1774 and 1775, a group of **delegates** met in Philadelphia, Pennsylvania. Most wanted the British to change laws that hurt the colonies. When Great Britain refused, the delegates declared independence. But King George did not let the colonies go without a fight. The Revolutionary War would rage for seven years.

Regular life did not stop during this time. Most children learned to read and write. Parents tended their farms and businesses. Families went to church. Still, many colonists made great **sacrifices** for independence. Some even lost their lives.

CHAPTER 2

EDUCATION

Colonial children learned reading, writing, and **arithmetic** in school. Learning to write came several years after reading. Arithmetic was learned even later.

Children who lived on farms miles from any village or town were taught to

LEARN MORE HERE!

Harvard University was founded as Harvard College in 1636. It was named after English colonist and pastor, John Harvard.

read by their parents. Many children who lived in villages or towns went to dame schools. A village woman, or "dame," was paid a small fee to teach children to read in her kitchen.

Depending on where a child lived, the only schooling he or she received was a few years at dame school. Boys sometimes went on to study at schools taught by schoolmasters. A schoolmaster, or teacher, was usually a strict man. Students

READING FOR FREEDOM

Thousands of pamphlets, or small books, were published in the years before and during the Revolutionary War. The most famous one was Thomas Paine's *Common Sense*. It spelled out the reasons America declared independence from Great Britain.

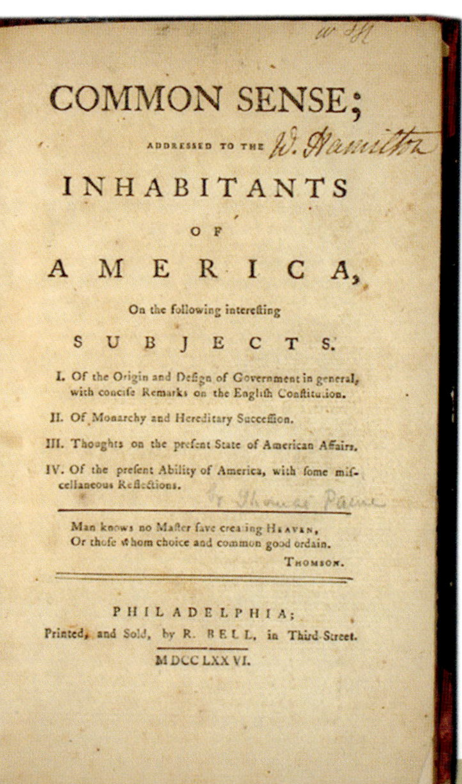
COMMON SENSE;

ADDRESSED TO THE

INHABITANTS

OF

AMERICA,

On the following interesting

SUBJECTS.

I. Of the Origin and Design of Government in general, with concise Remarks on the English Constitution.

II. Of Monarchy and Hereditary Succession.

III. Thoughts on the present State of American Affairs.

IV. Of the present Ability of America, with some miscellaneous Reflections.

Man knows no Master save creating HEAVEN,
Or those whom choice and common good ordain.

THOMSON.

PHILADELPHIA;
Printed, and Sold, by R. BELL, in Third Street.

MDCCLXXVI.

often said their lessons aloud, which made the schoolroom noisy. Girls were rarely allowed to attend those schools.

This illustration depicts how a one-room schoolhouse may have looked around the time of the Revolutionary War.

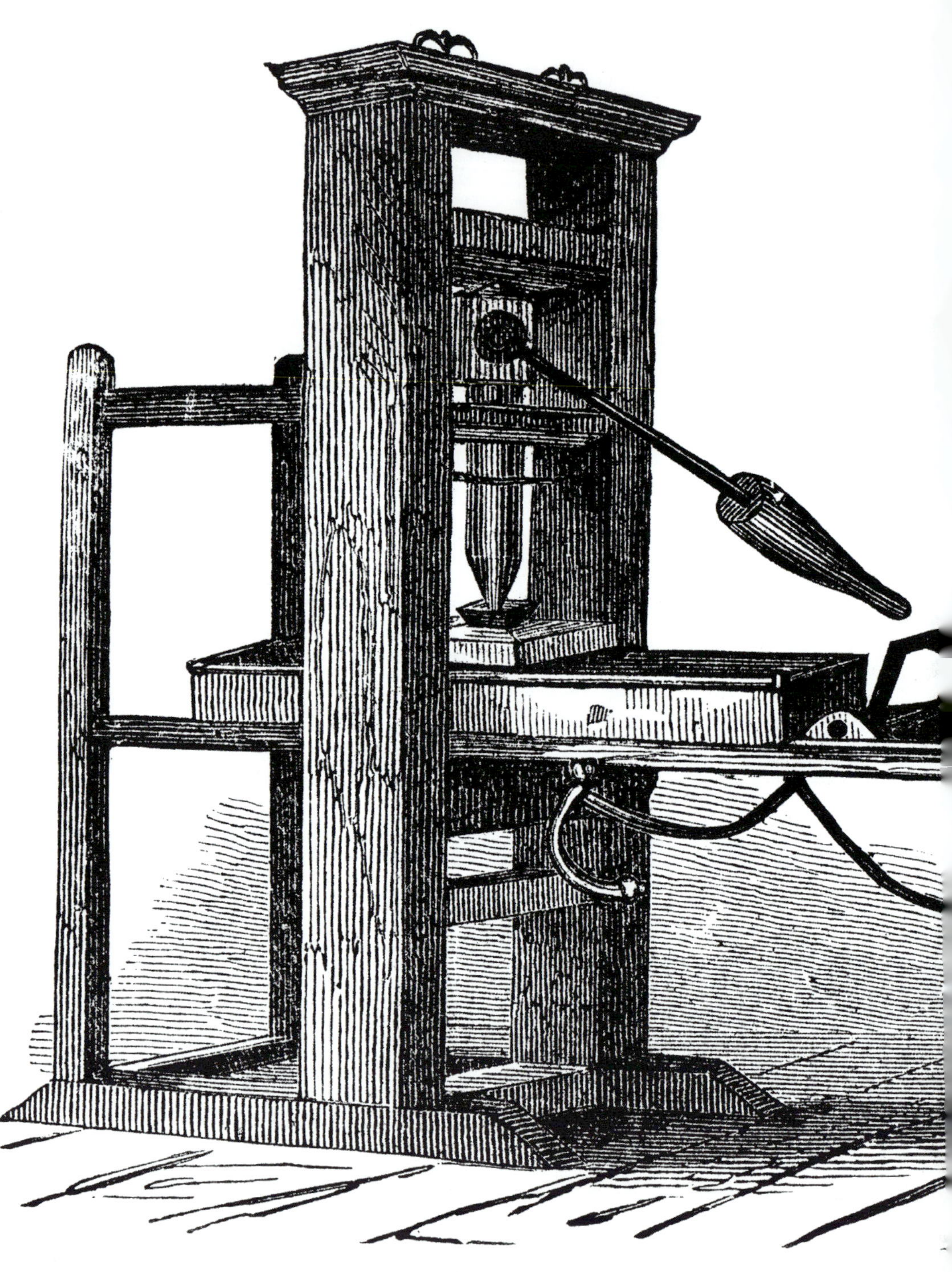

However, this began to change around the time of the Revolutionary War. Citizens of the newly formed United States needed to be informed so they could understand the new changes happening. More girls between the ages of six and eight were allowed to learn to read and write. Many Americans believed an education would help the United States become a strong nation.

An illustration of the printing press known for having printed the Declaration of Independence.

CHAPTER 3

WORK DURING WARTIME

The first American colonists were farmers. As the colonies grew, farmers learned new skills that were needed in their communities. At the time of the Revolutionary War, there were 35 listed trades one could learn. These included

EXPLORE LINKS HERE!

tailor, miller, and silversmith. Professional jobs existed too. These were lawyers, doctors, and ministers.

Colonial blacksmiths quickly forged weapons at the start of the Revolutionary War.

Women did not officially work at jobs during the Revolutionary War. But they did many of the same jobs as men, serving as helpers. Farm women could do almost everything their husbands did. When their husbands left to join the army, women took over running the farms. Wealthier women ran large households.

During the war, colonists **boycotted** all British-made goods. Women were the biggest reason the boycotts were

DID YOU KNOW?

Even wealthy women, such as Deborah Franklin, wife of politician Benjamin Franklin, made her family's clothing to show support for the colonies.

Spinning yarn at home was a way to protest the laws of Great Britain.

successful. They refused to purchase any kind of fabric imported from Great Britain. They organized all-day sewing events and wore clothing made of homespun cloth.

Men, women, and children all had important duties to keep their homes and communities running smoothly.

Children also worked. Girls usually helped their mothers with chores. A girl as young as four might help care for her siblings. Older boys worked on farms, in shops, or in workshops. Younger boys fed chickens, swept, and ran errands.

Though there was much work to be done during the Revolutionary War years, both children and adults found time to do joyful things. They played games and went to parties.

A popular game in colonial times was hoop rolling.

CHAPTER 4

SOLDIERING ON

The Second Continental Congress established the Continental Army in June of 1775. George Washington was made commander-in-chief. Members of this army were volunteers. As many as 150,000 served over the course of the war.

COMPLETE AN ACTIVITY HERE!

French officers and soldiers fought alongside Washington's army in the Revolutionary War.

enlistments could last anywhere from six months to three years. They were paid for their time with money or land.

Minutemen were trained in weaponry and military strategy. They were known for being ready to fight at a minute's notice.

Men from every colony joined the Continental Army. Most soldiers were between the ages of 15 and 30. But boys and older men also served.

Drummer boys were responsible for the army drums. They beat out different rhythms to tell soldiers what to do. This was important since shouted commands would be hard to hear in the noise of battle.

Drummer boys could be as young as 12 but were more often between the ages of 16 and 20.

This painting depicts General Cornwallis surrendering his army and sword to General George Washington.

Though soldiers fought in many battles, most died from diseases such as **smallpox** and **typhus**. Poor diet and dirty living conditions were to blame.

The Battle of Yorktown was the last battle of the Revolutionary War. Troops fought from September 28 to October 19 of 1781. British army general Charles Cornwallis surrendered to General George Washington. This led to a Continental Army victory and the official independence of a young nation.

A DAY IN THE LIFE

Marie has a baby, toddlers, a farm, and a home to care for on her own. Her husband left months ago to fight the war.

5:00 AM

Marie wakes and quickly mixes five loaves of bread and lets them rise. She feeds the baby. She throws down hay for the horses and lets the chickens out of the coop.

7:00 AM

Marie feeds the toddlers milk and yesterday's bread for breakfast. She adds wood to the fire to heat the oven to bake the dough she prepared earlier. She picks beans from the garden while the bread bakes.

9:00 AM

Marie feeds the baby again and mends the toddlers' clothes. She puts a pot of stew on the fire to cook for supper and takes the children along to fix a broken fence post. They pick blackberries on the way back to the house.

12:00 PM

Marie feeds the toddlers milk and cheese for lunch. She shells beans from the garden to add to the stew. She tends the garden and collects eggs from the chicken coop.

5:00 PM

Marie feeds the baby again. She milks the cows again and sets the milk to cool for churning into butter in the morning. She feeds the chickens corn and puts the horses in the shed for the night.

7:00 PM

The family sits down for supper. Marie then puts all the children to bed. She washes the dishes and sweeps the kitchen floor. She writes a letter to her husband. Finally, she reads the Bible and goes to bed.

MAKING CONNECTIONS

TEXT-TO-SELF

After reading this book, what do you think life would have been like for you if you were alive during the Revolutionary War?

TEXT-TO-TEXT

Have you read any other books about what life was like during the Revolutionary War? Did you learn any new information from those books?

TEXT-TO-WORLD

How did America's independence after the Revolutionary War change or affect other parts of the world?

GLOSSARY

arithmetic — the method of using whole numbers to add, subtract, multiply, and divide.

boycott — to refuse to buy, use, or go to, in order to make a protest or bring about change.

delegate — a person who is chosen to speak or act for others.

sacrifice — the act of giving up something of value.

smallpox — a contagious disease characterized by a fever and pus-filled pimples that often leave scars.

taxes — a sum of money paid to a government, which the government uses to pay for its services to the people and to maintain itself.

typhus — a serious illness that is spread by fleas, mites, and lice, and is marked by high fever, headache, and a red rash.

INDEX

This book is filled with videos, puzzles, games, and more! Scan the QR codes* while you read, or visit the website below to make this book pop.

popbooksonline.com/rev-war-life

*Scanning QR codes requires a web-enabled smart device with a QR code reader app and a camera.